how2become

KS2 MATHS IS EASY

(FRACTIONS, DECIMALS AND PERCENTAGES)

THE
REVISION
SERIES

www.How2Become.com

As part of this product you have also received FREE access to online tests that will help you to pass Key Stage 2 MATHS *(Fractions, Decimals and Percentages).*

To gain access, simply go to:

www.PsychometricTestsOnline.co.uk

Get more products for passing any test or interview at:

www.how2become.com

Orders: Please contact How2become Ltd, Suite 2, 50 Churchill Square Business Centre, Kings Hill, Kent ME19 4YU.

You can order through Amazon.co.uk under ISBN 9781910602430, via the website www.How2Become.com or through Gardners.com.

ISBN: 9781910602430

First published in 2015 by How2become Ltd.

Typeset for How2become Ltd by Anton Pshinka.

Disclaimer

Every effort has been made to ensure that the information contained within this guide is accurate at the time of publication. How2become Ltd are not responsible for anyone failing any part of any selection process as a result of the information contained within this guide. How2become Ltd and their authors cannot accept any responsibility for any errors or omissions within this guide, however caused. No responsibility for loss or damage occasioned by any person acting, or refraining from action, as a result of the material in this publication can be accepted by How2become Ltd.

The information within this guide does not represent the views of any third party service or organisation.

CONTENTS

THE
REVISION
SERIES

UNDERSTANDING FRACTIONS

UNDERSTANDING FRACTIONS

DEFINITION

A fraction is PART of a whole number.

A FRACTION is made up of 2 numbers.

$\frac{2}{5}$
$2 \longrightarrow$ The top number is called the NUMERATOR.
$5 \longrightarrow$ The bottom number is called the DENOMINATOR.

THE NUMERATOR

The numerator number tells you how many 'bits' we are <u>trying to work out.</u>

THE DENOMINATOR

The denominator number tells you how many bits there are <u>'altogether'.</u>

EXAMPLE

$$\frac{2}{5} =$$

So in the above example, we know that the fraction is referring to '2' parts of the '5' in total.

<u>Let's put this in context:</u>

Sam has 5 cats (the number altogether i.e. 'the denominator'). 2 of Sam's cats have fleas (the part you are trying to work out i.e. 'the numerator'). This can be shown as the fraction $\frac{2}{5}$ (i.e. 2 out of 5).

<u>Let's try another context:</u>

There are 5 chickens in total. 2 of the chickens have laid eggs. This can be shown as the fraction $\frac{2}{5}$ (i.e. 2 out of 5).

Question 1

For the following fraction, come up with a possible context:

$$\frac{3}{9}$$

Question 2

For the following fraction, come up with a possible context:

$$\frac{7}{11}$$

Question 3

For the following fraction, come up with a possible context:

$$\frac{1}{8}$$

Question 4

For the following fraction, come up with a possible context:

$$\frac{11}{17}$$

Question 5

For the following fraction, come up with a possible context:

$$\frac{27}{31}$$

Question 6

For the following fraction, come up with a possible context:

$$\frac{5}{9}$$

ANSWERS TO UNDERSTANDING FRACTIONS

> ### *Please note*
>
> *For these questions, you could have used **any** context that you wanted to, so long as you used the numbers in the correct way.*

Q1. $\dfrac{3}{9}$

In a classroom there were 9 pupils, and 3 of them were boys.

Q2. $\dfrac{7}{11}$

In a field, there are 11 sheep. 7 of the sheep have been sheered.

Q3. $\dfrac{1}{8}$

A bag contained 8 buttons. 1 of the buttons is pink.

Q4. $\dfrac{11}{17}$

In a class, there were 17 pupils in total. 11 of the pupils achieved golden stars for good behaviour.

Q5. $\dfrac{27}{31}$

There are 31 days in January. Out of the 31 days, 27 of those days were rainy.

Q6. $\dfrac{5}{9}$

Elliott has 9 homework assignments in one week. Out of the 9, he has completed 5 of his homework assignments.

HOW ARE YOU GETTING ON?

THE REVISION SERIES

FRACTIONS OF SHAPES

FRACTIONS OF SHAPES

FRACTIONS OF SHAPES

Remember, a fraction has 2 parts – the top number, and the bottom number.

Finding the fraction of a shape will depend on how many parts the shape is being broken in to, and the 'parts' you are trying to find out.

EXAMPLE 1

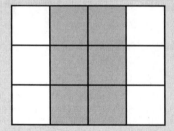 $= \dfrac{1}{2}$

- As you can see, there are 2 squares in total. (So, the '2' will form the bottom part of the fraction).

- 1 of the squares is shaded. So this represents '1 out of 2'. This can be written as $\dfrac{1}{2}$.

EXAMPLE 2

- There are 12 squares in total.

- 6 squares are shaded. So this represents '6 out of 12'. This can be written as $\dfrac{6}{12}$.

- This can also be **simplified** to $\dfrac{1}{2}$, which will be discussed in a later chapter.

Question 1

What fraction of the shape is shaded?

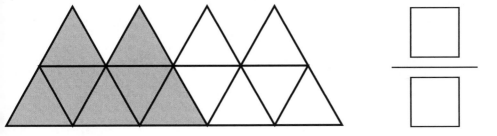

Question 2

What fraction of the shape is shaded?

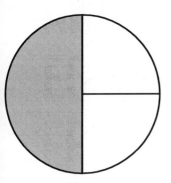

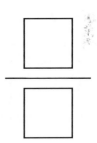

Question 3

What fraction of the shape is shaded?

Question 4

What fraction of the shape is shaded?

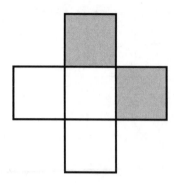

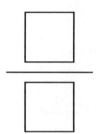

Question 5

Shade in $\frac{3}{8}$ of the shape.

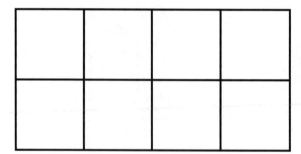

Question 6

Shade in $\frac{1}{3}$ of the shape.

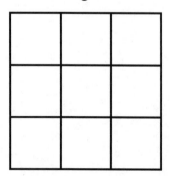

Question 7

Shade in $\frac{5}{8}$ of the shape.

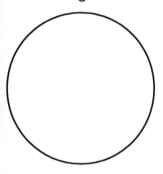

Question 8

Shade in $\frac{1}{4}$ of the shape.

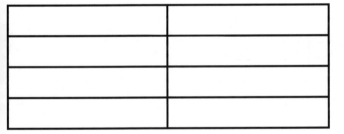

Question 9

Shade in $\frac{1}{3}$ of the shape.

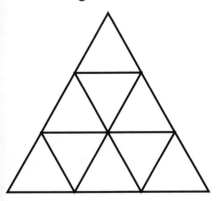

ANSWERS TO FRACTIONS OF SHAPES

Q1. $\dfrac{7}{13}$

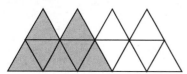

Q2. $\dfrac{1}{2}$

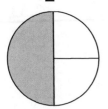

Q3. $\dfrac{1}{5}$

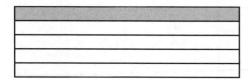

Q4. $\dfrac{2}{5}$

Q5. 3 out of the 8 squares need to be shaded in.

Q6. 3 of the 9 squares need to be shaded in. ($\frac{3}{9}$ is the same as $\frac{1}{3}$).

Q7. 5 segments of the circle need to be shaded in.

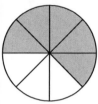

Q8. 2 out of the 8 squares need to be shaded in. ($\frac{2}{8}$ is the same as $\frac{1}{4}$).

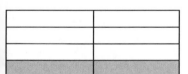

Q9. 3 out of the 9 triangles need to be shaded in. ($\frac{3}{9}$ is the same as $\frac{1}{3}$).

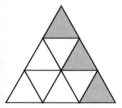

HOW ARE YOU GETTING ON?

THE
REVISION
SERIES

SIMPLIFYING AND EQUIVALENT FRACTIONS

SIMPLIFYING FRACTIONS

SIMPLIFYING FRACTIONS

The word SIMPLIFYING simply means 'to make it simple'. Sometimes, you can simplify fractions in order to make them easier to understand.

TIP

You can simplify fractions by one easy method. Make the fraction simple by dividing the numerator and the denominator by the same number.

EXAMPLE

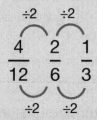

REMEMBER!

TIP

You need to find a number that both of the numbers can be divided by. Sometimes fractions will simplify more than once.

Try this!

Simplify $\dfrac{15}{20}$

Did you get the right answer? Let's see!

Step 1 = find a number that both 15 and 20 can be divided by. Both numbers are multiples of 5.

Step 2 = $15 \div 5 = 3$, and $20 \div 5 = 4$. This makes the new fraction of $\dfrac{3}{4}$.

EQUIVALENT FRACTIONS

Equivalent = 'the same as'.

So, equivalent fractions look different, but are actually representing the same thing. As in the previous examples of simplifying, you are looking for a new way to write a fraction in order to make it easier to understand.

FRACTION BARS

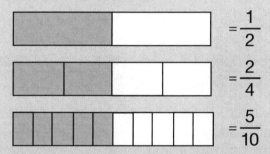

$$= \frac{1}{2}$$

$$= \frac{2}{4}$$

$$= \frac{5}{10}$$

As you can see, the above fraction bars demonstrate the same amount being shaded in, but they are just written in a different way. Obviously $\frac{1}{2}$ is easier to understand than $\frac{5}{10}$, but they do mean the same!

• You can make equivalent fractions by multiplying or dividing the top AND bottom number, by the SAME number.

Now you try!

What is the equivalent to $\frac{30}{42}$? Cancel down the fraction until you find the simplest form.

Question 1

Below there are 10 cards. Each card has a fraction on it. Match the boxes from the top row to the bottom row that have the same value. The first one has been done for you.

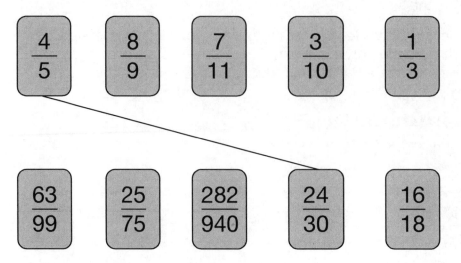

Question 2

Which of the following fractions is the same as $\frac{3}{9}$? Please circle your answer.

A	B	C	D
$\frac{1}{2}$	$\frac{6}{12}$	$\frac{1}{3}$	$\frac{9}{29}$

Question 3

Which of the following fractions is the same as $\frac{4}{5}$? Please circle your answer.

A	B	C	D
$\frac{1}{5}$	$\frac{1}{2}$	$\frac{2}{3}$	Already in its simplest form

Question 4

Complete the following fractions by making them equivalent to the fraction $\frac{3}{7}$.

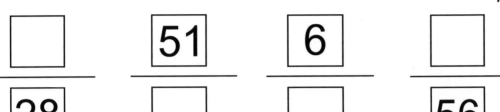

Question 5

Sam has a birthday party. His cake has been divided into 12 pieces. Out of the 12 pieces, 8 pieces get eaten. Write the fraction, in its simplest form, of the amount of cake LEFT.

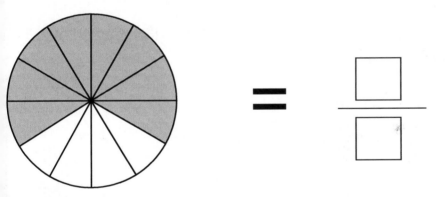

Question 6

Below is a bar. Break up the fraction bar which shows $\frac{7}{28}$ in its simplest

form. Shade in the correct amount.

ANSWERS TO SIMPLIFYING AND EQUIVALENT FRACTIONS

Q1. Your answer should look something like this:

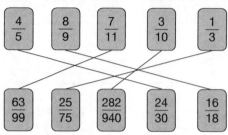

Q2. $C = \dfrac{1}{3}$

EXPLANATION = $\dfrac{3}{9}$ can be simplified to $\dfrac{1}{3}$ Both numbers can be divided by 3.

Q3. D = Already in its simplest form.

EXPLANATION = $\dfrac{4}{5}$ is already in its simplest form. There is no number that can be divided by 4 and 5. (5 is a prime number).

Q4. Your answer should look like this:

$\dfrac{12}{28}$ $\dfrac{51}{119}$ $\dfrac{6}{14}$ $\dfrac{24}{56}$

Q5. $\dfrac{1}{3}$

EXPLANATION = the cake is cut into 12 pieces. 8 pieces get eaten, therefore leaving 4 pieces of cake left. So this can be written as a fraction $\dfrac{4}{12}$. This can be simplified to $\dfrac{1}{3}$. Both numbers can be divided by 4.

Q6. Your answer should look something like this:

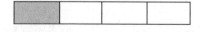

HOW ARE YOU GETTING ON?

THE
REVISION
SERIES

ADDING AND SUBTRACTING FRACTIONS

ADDING AND SUBTRACTING FRACTIONS

ADDING FRACTIONS

There is a simple way to add and subtract fractions. Use the following method below for any question relating to adding or subtracting fractions.

'CROSSBOW METHOD'

$$\frac{3}{4} + \frac{2}{5} = \frac{15+8}{20} = \frac{23}{20} = 1\frac{3}{20}$$

Draw two diagonal lines through both of the fractions as shown. (This forms the CROSS which looks like a multiplication sign).

It tells you to multiply the 3 by 5 = 15
It tells you to multiply the 4 by 2 = 8.

Then draw your BOW (from the bottom number of the first fraction to the bottom number of the second fraction).

Again, multiply these two numbers: 4 x 5 = 20

SUBTRACTING FRACTIONS

PLEASE NOTE: the same method applies when subtracting, but instead of adding the two numbers that form the top part of the fraction, you minus them.

$$\frac{4}{7} - \frac{1}{3} = \frac{12-7}{21} = \frac{5}{21}$$

Draw two diagonal lines through both of the fractions as shown. (This forms the CROSS which looks like a multiplication sign).

It tells you to multiply the 4 by 3 = 12
It tells you to multiply the 7 by 1 = 7. 12 - 7 = 5

Then draw your BOW (from the bottom number of the first fraction to the bottom number of the second fraction).

Again, multiply these two numbers: 7 x 3 = 21

Question 1

$$\frac{2}{7} + \frac{3}{7} = \frac{\Box}{\Box}$$

Question 2

$$\frac{8}{10} - \frac{1}{4} = \frac{\Box}{\Box}$$

Question 3

$$\frac{5}{8} + \frac{3}{4} = \frac{\Box}{\Box}$$

Question 4

$$\frac{5}{9} - \frac{3}{9} = \frac{\Box}{\Box}$$

Question 5

$$\frac{2}{6} + \frac{2}{3} = \frac{\Box}{\Box}$$

Question 6

$$\frac{3}{4} - \frac{1}{2} = \frac{\Box}{\Box}$$

Question 7

$$\frac{5}{13} - \frac{4}{13} = \frac{\Box}{\Box}$$

Question 8

$$\frac{6}{11} + \frac{4}{13} = \frac{\Box}{\Box}$$

Question 9

$$2\frac{5}{6} + \frac{2}{4} = \frac{\square}{\square}$$

Question 10

$$\frac{2}{7} + \frac{9}{10} = \frac{\square}{\square}$$

Question 11

$$1\frac{6}{7} - \frac{2}{3} = \frac{\square}{\square}$$

Question 12

$$\frac{4}{5} - \frac{2}{3} = \frac{\square}{\square}$$

Question 13

$$\frac{8}{11} - \frac{2}{4} = \frac{\square}{\square}$$

Question 14

$$\frac{7}{12} + 1\frac{3}{7} = \frac{\square}{\square}$$

Question 15

$$2\frac{3}{4} - \frac{4}{13} = \frac{\square}{\square}$$

Question 16

$$\frac{6}{11} + \frac{4}{13} = \frac{\square}{\square}$$

ANSWERS TO ADDING AND SUBTRACTING FRACTIONS

Q1. $\dfrac{5}{7}$

EXPLANATION $= \dfrac{2}{7} + \dfrac{3}{7} = \dfrac{5}{7}$

Q2. $\dfrac{22}{40} = \dfrac{11}{20}$

EXPLANATION $= \dfrac{8}{10} \times \dfrac{1}{4} = \dfrac{32-10}{40} = \dfrac{22}{40} = \dfrac{11}{20}$

Q3. $\dfrac{44}{32} = \dfrac{11}{8} = 1\dfrac{3}{8}$

EXPLANATION $= \dfrac{5}{8} + \dfrac{3}{4} = \dfrac{20+24}{32} = \dfrac{44}{32} = \dfrac{11}{8} = 1\dfrac{3}{8}$

Q4. $\dfrac{2}{9}$

EXPLANATION $= \dfrac{5}{9} - \dfrac{3}{9} = \dfrac{2}{9}$

Q5. $\dfrac{18}{18} = \dfrac{1}{1} = 1$

EXPLANATION $= \dfrac{2}{6} + \dfrac{2}{3} = \dfrac{6+12}{18} = \dfrac{18}{18} = \dfrac{1}{1} = 1$

Q6. $\dfrac{2}{8} = \dfrac{1}{4}$

EXPLANATION $= \dfrac{3}{4} \times \dfrac{1}{2} = \dfrac{6-4}{8} = \dfrac{2}{8} = \dfrac{1}{4}$

Q7. $\dfrac{1}{13}$

EXPLANATION $= \dfrac{5}{13} - \dfrac{4}{13} = \dfrac{1}{13}$

Q8. $\dfrac{122}{143}$

EXPLANATION $= \dfrac{6}{11} + \dfrac{4}{13} = \dfrac{78+44}{143} = \dfrac{122}{143}$

Q9. $\dfrac{80}{24} = 3\dfrac{8}{24} = 3\dfrac{1}{3}$

EXPLANATION $= 2\dfrac{5}{6} + \dfrac{2}{4} = \dfrac{17}{6} + \dfrac{2}{4} = \dfrac{68+12}{24} = \dfrac{80}{24} = 3\dfrac{8}{24} = 3\dfrac{1}{3}$

Q10. $\dfrac{83}{70} = 1\dfrac{13}{70}$

EXPLANATION $= \dfrac{2}{7} + \dfrac{9}{10} = \dfrac{20+63}{70} = \dfrac{83}{70} = 1\dfrac{13}{70}$

Q11. $\dfrac{25}{21} = 1\dfrac{4}{21}$

EXPLANATION $= 1\dfrac{6}{7} - \dfrac{2}{3} = \dfrac{13}{7} - \dfrac{2}{3} = \dfrac{39-14}{21} = \dfrac{25}{21} = 1\dfrac{4}{21}$

Q12. $\dfrac{2}{15}$

EXPLANATION $= \dfrac{4}{5} - \dfrac{2}{3} = \dfrac{12-10}{15} = \dfrac{2}{15}$

Q13. $\dfrac{10}{44} = \dfrac{5}{22}$

EXPLANATION $= \dfrac{8}{11} \diagdown \dfrac{2}{4} = \dfrac{32-22}{44} = \dfrac{10}{44} = \dfrac{5}{22}$

Q14. $\dfrac{169}{84} = 2\dfrac{1}{84}$

EXPLANATION $= \dfrac{7}{12} + 1\dfrac{3}{7} = \dfrac{7}{12} + \dfrac{10}{7} = \dfrac{49+120}{84} = \dfrac{169}{84} = 2\dfrac{1}{84}$

Q15. $\dfrac{159}{52} = 3\dfrac{3}{52}$

EXPLANATION $= 2\dfrac{3}{4} - \dfrac{4}{13} = \dfrac{11}{4} + \dfrac{4}{13} = \dfrac{143+16}{52} = \dfrac{159}{52} = 3\dfrac{3}{52}$

Q16. $\dfrac{122}{143}$

EXPLANATION $= \dfrac{6}{11} + \dfrac{4}{13} = \dfrac{78+44}{143} = \dfrac{122}{143}$

HOW ARE YOU GETTING ON?

MULTIPLYING AND DIVIDING FRACTIONS

MULTIPLYING AND DIVIDING FRACTIONS

MULTIPLYING FRACTIONS

There is a very easy way to multiply fractions.

'ARROW METHOD'

$$\frac{5}{9} \times \frac{3}{5} = \frac{15}{45} = \frac{3}{9} = \frac{1}{3}$$

Draw an arrow through the two top numbers and multiply.
5 x 3 = 15

Draw an arrow through the two bottom numbers.
9 x 5 = 45

Done! (Some fractions will be able to be simplified, as shown in above example).

Remember = if you have a whole number and you need to multiply, you will need to convert this to a fraction. This is really simple, just place a 1 underneath, to form the bottom part of the fraction

EXAMPLE

$$4 = \frac{4}{1}$$

DIVIDING FRACTIONS

$$\frac{4}{7} \div \frac{3}{4} = \frac{4}{7} \times \frac{4}{3} = \frac{16}{21}$$

This is actually quite simple. Turn the second fraction upside down. Change the divide sum to a multiply, and then use the SAME method as if you were multiplying.

You will get the answer correct every time!

Question 1

$$\frac{1}{4} \times 24 = \frac{\square}{\square}$$

Question 2

$$\frac{5}{8} \times 32 = \frac{\square}{\square}$$

Question 3

$$\frac{1}{2} \div 4 = \frac{\square}{\square}$$

Question 4

$$\frac{2}{3} \times \frac{6}{7} = \frac{\square}{\square}$$

Question 5

$$2\frac{4}{5} \times 15 = \frac{\square}{\square}$$

Question 6

$$1\frac{1}{4} \times 48 = \frac{\square}{\square}$$

Question 7

$$\frac{7}{11} \times \frac{3}{8} = \frac{\square}{\square}$$

Question 8

$$\frac{2}{8} \div 2 = \frac{\square}{\square}$$

Question 9

$$\frac{1}{12} \times \frac{1}{6} = \frac{\Box}{\Box}$$

Question 10

$$\frac{1}{3} \times 21 = \frac{\Box}{\Box}$$

Question 11

$$\frac{3}{9} \div \frac{1}{3} = \frac{\Box}{\Box}$$

Question 12

$$\frac{1}{2} \times \frac{3}{4} = \frac{\Box}{\Box}$$

Question 13

$$\frac{3}{100} \div 10 = \frac{\Box}{\Box}$$

Question 14

$$\frac{7}{10} \div 10 = \frac{\Box}{\Box}$$

Question 15

$$\frac{3}{8} \times \frac{11}{14} = \frac{\Box}{\Box}$$

Question 16

$$\frac{3}{5} \div 6 = \frac{\Box}{\Box}$$

ANSWERS TO MULTIPLYING AND DIVIDING FRACTIONS

Q1. 6

EXPLANATION $= \dfrac{1}{4} \times \dfrac{24}{1} = \dfrac{24}{4} = \dfrac{6}{1} = 6$

Q2. 20

EXPLANATION $= \dfrac{5}{8} \times \dfrac{32}{1} = \dfrac{160}{8} = \dfrac{20}{1} = 20$

Q3. $\dfrac{1}{8}$

EXPLANATION $= \dfrac{1}{2} \div \dfrac{4}{1} = \dfrac{1}{2} \times \dfrac{1}{4} = \dfrac{1}{8}$

Q4. $\dfrac{12}{21} = \dfrac{4}{7}$

EXPLANATION $= \dfrac{2}{3} \times \dfrac{6}{7} = \dfrac{12}{21} = \dfrac{4}{7}$

Q5. 42

EXPLANATION $= 2\dfrac{4}{5} \times 15 = \dfrac{14}{5} \times \dfrac{15}{1} = \dfrac{210}{5} = \dfrac{42}{1} = 42$

Q6. 60

EXPLANATION $= 1\dfrac{1}{4} \times 48 = \dfrac{5}{4} \times \dfrac{48}{1} = \dfrac{240}{4} = \dfrac{60}{1} = 60$

Q7. $\dfrac{21}{88}$

EXPLANATION $= \dfrac{\cancel{7}}{\cancel{11}} \times \dfrac{\cancel{3}}{\cancel{8}} = \dfrac{21}{88}$

Q8. $\dfrac{2}{16} = \dfrac{1}{8}$

EXPLANATION $= \dfrac{2}{8} \div 2 = \dfrac{2}{8} \div \dfrac{2}{1} = \dfrac{2}{8} \times \dfrac{1}{2} = \dfrac{2}{16} = \dfrac{1}{8}$

Q9. $\dfrac{1}{72}$

EXPLANATION $= \dfrac{1}{12} \times \dfrac{1}{6} = \dfrac{1}{72}$

Q10. $\dfrac{21}{3} = 7$

EXPLANATION $= \dfrac{1}{3} \times \dfrac{21}{1} = \dfrac{21}{3} = 7$

Q11. $\dfrac{9}{9} = 1$

EXPLANATION $= \dfrac{3}{9} \div \dfrac{1}{3} = \dfrac{3}{9} \times \dfrac{3}{1} = \dfrac{9}{9} = \dfrac{1}{1} = 1$

Q12. $\dfrac{3}{8}$

EXPLANATION $= \dfrac{1}{2} \times \dfrac{3}{4} = \dfrac{3}{8}$

Q13. $\dfrac{3}{1000}$

EXPLANATION $= \dfrac{3}{100} \div \dfrac{10}{1} = \dfrac{3}{100} \times \dfrac{1}{10} = \dfrac{3}{1000}$

Q14. $\dfrac{7}{100}$

EXPLANATION $= \dfrac{7}{10} \div \dfrac{10}{1} = \dfrac{7}{10} \times \dfrac{1}{10} = \dfrac{7}{100}$

Q15. $\dfrac{33}{112}$

EXPLANATION $= \dfrac{3}{8} \times \dfrac{11}{14} = \dfrac{33}{112}$

Q16. $\dfrac{3}{30} = \dfrac{1}{10}$

EXPLANATION $= \dfrac{3}{5} \div \dfrac{6}{1} = \dfrac{3}{5} \times \dfrac{1}{6} = \dfrac{3}{30} = \dfrac{1}{10}$

HOW ARE YOU GETTING ON?

THE
REVISION
SERIES

UNDERSTANDING DECIMALS

UNDERSTANDING DECIMALS

DEFINITION

Like fractions, decimals are another way of writing a number that is not whole.

A decimal is in fact 'in-between numbers'.

EXAMPLE

6.48 ⟶ This is in between the number 6 and the number 7.

USING PLACE VALUES

In order to work out what the decimal is representing, you should use **place values.**

These include: ***units, tenths, hundredths*** and ***thousandths***.

- Using the above example of 6.48, let's place these under the sub-headings.

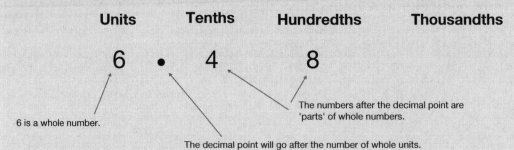

Units	**Tenths**	**Hundredths**	**Thousandths**
6 •	4	8	

The numbers after the decimal point are 'parts' of whole numbers.

6 is a whole number.

The decimal point will go after the number of whole units.

When it comes to decimals, an important thing to remember is the decimal point. If you are adding or subtracting, you need to make sure that the decimals are added in the correct columns.

TIP

- Make sure you begin with writing the decimal points so they are directly beneath one another, and then fill in the numbers. That way you know the numbers will all be in the correct column when it comes to doing the sum.

Question 1

Write the following decimal under the correct place value headings.

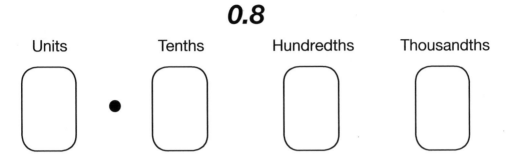

Question 2

Write the following decimal under the correct place value headings.

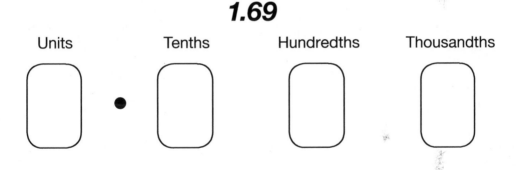

Question 3

Write the following decimal under the correct place value headings.

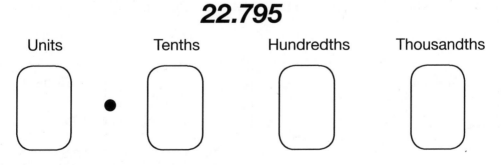

Question 4

Below is a number line. Write the missing numbers in the boxes provided.

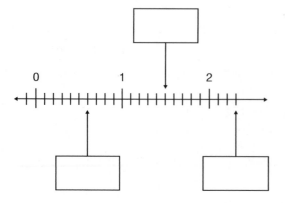

Question 5

Below is a number line. Write the missing numbers in the boxes provided.

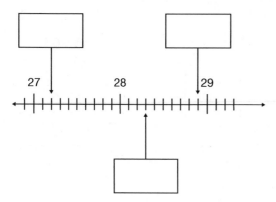

Question 6

Put these decimals in order from smallest to biggest.

| 0.2 | 0.02 | 0.215 | 0.05 |

Smallest			Biggest

ANSWERS TO UNDERSTANDING DECIMALS

Q1. Your answer should look like this:

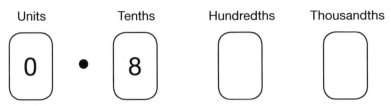

Units		Tenths	Hundredths	Thousandths
0	•	8		

Q2. Your answer should look like this:

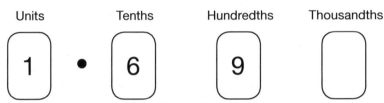

Units		Tenths	Hundredths	Thousandths
1	•	6	9	

Q3. Your answer should look like this:

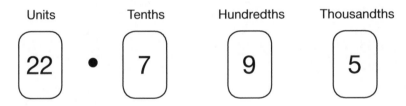

Units		Tenths	Hundredths	Thousandths
22	•	7	9	5

Q4. 0.6, 1.5, 2.3

EXPLANATION = the lines in between each whole number represents point 1.

Q5. 27.2, 28.3, 28.9

EXPLANATION = the lines in between each whole number represents point 1.

Q6. 0.02, 0.05, 0.2, 0.215

EXPLANATION = from smallest to biggest, you need to pay attention to the units, tenths, hundredths and thousandths.

HOW ARE YOU GETTING ON?

ADDING
AND
SUBTRACTING
DECIMALS

ADDING AND SUBTRACTING DECIMALS

HOW TO ADD DECIMALS

- To add decimals, you need to line up the decimal points.

EXAMPLE

0.5 + 0.62

How to work it out:

$$\begin{array}{r} 0.5 \\ +\ 0.62 \\ \hline 1.12 \end{array}$$

The decimal points need to be lined up!

Your answer should begin by adding the decimal point in first, and then add up the columns from left to right.

HOW TO SUBTRACT DECIMALS

- Again, as you did for adding decimals, you will need to line up the decimal points and then subtract each column (starting from the left).

2.46 - 1.35

How to work it out:

$$\begin{array}{r} 2.46 \\ -\ 1.35 \\ \hline 1.11 \end{array}$$

The decimal points need to be lined up!

Your answer should begin by adding the decimal point in first, and then subtracting the columns from left to right.

Question 1

Work out the following sum.

6.12 + 7.4192

Question 2

Work out the following sum.

986.345 – 123.46

Question 3

Work out the following sum.

8.6958 + 423.23

Question 4

Work out the following sum.

9.3257 – 4.2156

Question 5

Work out the following sum.

41.26 + 98.745

Question 6

Work out the following sum.

558.42 − 551.42

Question 7

Work out the following sum.

0.00632 + 0.05387

Question 8

Work out the following sum.

5.00698 − 3.04879

ANSWERS TO ADDING AND SUBTRACTING DECIMALS

Q1. 13.5392

EXPLANATION = 6.12 + 7.4192 = 13.5392

Q2. 862.885

EXPLANATION = 986.345 − 123.46 = 862.885

Q3. 431.9258

EXPLANATION = 8.6958 + 423.23 = 431.9258

Q4. 5.1101

EXPLANATION = 9.3257 − 4.2156 = 5.1101

Q5. 140.005

EXPLANATION = 41.26 + 98.745 = 140.005

Q6. 7

EXPLANATION = 558.42 − 551.42 = 7

Q7. 0.06019

EXPLANATION = 0.00632 + 0.05387 = 0.06019

Q8. 1.95819

EXPLANATION = 5.00698 − 3.04879 = 1.95819

HOW ARE YOU GETTING ON?

THE
REVISION
SERIES

MULTIPLYING
AND
DIVIDING DECIMALS

MULTIPLYING DECIMALS

HOW TO MULTIPLY DECIMALS

- The easiest way to multiply decimals, is to remove the decimal point, do the multiplication, and then add in the decimal point at the end.

Note, if a decimal has a 0 that means there is nothing there. If a 0 begins or ends the number, you can remove these.

0.2 = 2
0.20 = 0.2

EXAMPLE

2.5 x 0.2

How to work it out:

- Remove the decimal points.

    25 x 2 = 50

- Now add in the decimal points. REMEMBER, you need to work out how many numbers come AFTER the decimal point in the question.

- You should notice that two numbers come after the decimal point (the .5 and the .2).

- Therefore 2 numbers need to come after the decimal point in the answer.

    25 x 2 = 50

- So the answer would be 0.50 or 0.5. It is usually written 0.5 (the 0 at the end is not necessary).

Now you try!

0.12 x 0.6

DIVIDING DECIMALS

HOW TO DIVIDE DECIMALS

*   Use the same method as we have just learned when multiplying decimals, but this time divide the two numbers instead of multiply.

EXAMPLE

REMEMBER: division is easy if you are dividing by whole numbers. You need to move the decimal points in both numbers the same number of places.

5.39 ÷ 1.1

How to work it out:

Move the decimal point 1 space.

53.9 ÷ 11.

*   Now ignore the decimal point in 53.9, do long division and then add it in at the end.

$$
\begin{array}{r}
049 \\
^{11}\overline{\smash{\big)}\,539} \\
5 \\
0 \\
\hline
53 \\
44 \\
\hline
99 \\
99 \\
\hline
0
\end{array}
$$

Put the decimal point in the answer directly above the decimal point in the question.

$$
^{11}\overline{\smash{\big)}\,53.9}^{\;04.9}
$$

ANSWER = 4.9

Now you try!

0.12 x 0.6

Question 1

Work out the following sum.

2.478 x 1.2

Question 2

Work out the following sum.

5.8 ÷ 0.2

Question 3

Work out the following sum.

2.10 ÷ 0.5

Question 4

Work out the following sum.

5.23 x 2.4

Question 5

Work out the following sum.

$8 \div 0.2$

Question 6

Work out the following sum.

$350 \div 0.25$

Question 7

Work out the following sum.

5.75×0.36

Question 8

Work out the following sum.

$7 \div 0.1$

ANSWERS TO MULTIPLYING AND DIVIDING DECIMALS

Q1. 2.9736

EXPLANATION = 2.478 x 1.2. Remove the decimal points, do the multiplication, and then add in the decimal points at the end. So, 2478 x 12 = 29736. Now add in the decimal point. There are four numbers that need to be after the decimal point (.478 and .2). So 29736 becomes 2.9736

Q2. 29

EXPLANATION = 5.8 ÷ 0.2. Remove the decimal points to make whole numbers, and then do the sum. 58 ÷ 2 = 29

Q3. 4.2

EXPLANATION = 2.10 ÷ 0.5. Remove the decimal points to make whole numbers, and then do the sum. 21 ÷ 5 = 4.2

Q4. 12.552

EXPLANATION = 5.23 x 2.4. Remove the decimal points, do the multiplication, and then add in the decimal points at the end. So, 523 x 24 = 12552. Now add in the decimal point. There are three numbers that need to be after the decimal point (.23 and .4). So 12552 becomes 12.552

Q5. 40

EXPLANATION = 8 ÷ 0.2. Remove the decimal points to make whole numbers, and then do the sum. 8 ÷ 0.2 = 40

Q6. 1400

EXPLANATION = 350 ÷ 0.25. Remove the decimal points to make whole numbers, and then do the sum. 350 ÷ 0.25 = 1400

Q7. 2.07

EXPLANATION = 5.75 x 0.36. Remove the decimal points, do the multiplication, and then add in the decimal points at the end. So, 575 x 36 = 20700. Now add in the decimal point. There are four numbers that need to be after the decimal point (.75 and .36). So 20700 becomes 2.0700 or 2.07

Q8. 70

EXPLANATION = 7 ÷ 0.1. Remove the decimal points to make whole numbers, and then do the sum. 7 ÷ 1 = 7. 0.1 is written in tenths, therefore 7 x 10 = 70

HOW ARE YOU GETTING ON?

THE
REVISION
SERIES

UNDERSTANDING
PERCENTAGES

UNDERSTANDING PERCENTAGES

UNDERSTANDING PERCENTAGES

Percentages are used to work out part of a number. For example 25% of something is equivalent to $\frac{1}{4}$ or 0.25

Per cent ⟶ out of 100

EXAMPLE

60% means 60 out of 100.
25% means 25 out of 100.

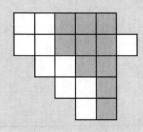

- To work out what percentage of this shape is shaded, you first need to work out the total number of squares.

Total number of squares = 20.

- Now work out the number of squares shaded.

Number of squares shaded = 10.

- There are 20 equal parts which means each square represents 5% (5 x 20 = 100). So, 5% x 10 (shaded squares) = 50%

PERCENTAGE OF A NUMBER

To work out the percentage of a number, i.e. 35% of 300, you should ALWAYS use the following method as it guarantees that you get the correct answer.

35% of 300

Step 1 = 300 ÷ 100 = 3

Step 2 = 3 x 35 = 105.

Step 3 = 105 is 35% of 300.

Alternatively, you can convert the percentage into a decimal. So 35% become 0.35 x 300 = 105.

Question 1

Work out the following sum.

30% of 150

Question 2

Work out the following sum.

75% of 400

Question 3

Work out the following sum.

18% of 200

Question 4

Work out the following sum.

62% of 1200

Question 5

Emma earns £300 in two weeks. She spends 30% of her earnings on clothes for her upcoming holiday. How much did Emma spend?

£220   £75   £115   £90   £100

Question 6

Shade in 20% of this shape.

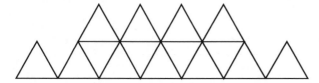

Question 7

What percentage of the large square below is shaded?

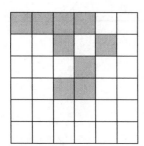

ANSWER

Question 8

Sammie is going to make chocolate peanut squares. There are just three ingredients, chocolate (40%), peanut butter (30%) and rice crispies (30%). How much of each ingredient will she need to make 900 g of mixture?

Chocolate =

Peanut Butter =

Rice Crispies =

ANSWERS TO UNDERSTANDING PERCENTAGES

Q1. 45

EXPLANATION = 150 ÷ 100 x 30 = 45

Q2. 300

EXPLANATION = 400 ÷ 100 x 75 = 300

Q3. 36

EXPLANATION = 200 ÷ 100 x 18 = 36

Q4. 744

EXPLANATION = 1200 ÷ 100 x 62 = 744

Q5. £90

EXPLANATION = £300 ÷ 100 x 30 = £90

Q6. Your answer should look something like this:

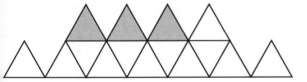

Q7. 25%

EXPLANATION = 9 squares are shaded in. There 36 squares in total. A quarter of the squares have been shaded in. The equivalent percentage to $\frac{1}{4}$ is 25%.

Q8. Chocolate = 360g, Peanut Butter = 270g, Rice Crispies = 270g.

EXPLANATION = to work out the chocolate: 900 ÷ 100 x 40 = 360g. To work out the peanut butter: 900 ÷ 100 x 30 = 270g. To work out the rice crispies: 900 ÷ 100 x 30 = 270g.

HOW ARE YOU GETTING ON?

THE
REVISION
SERIES

FRACTIONS INTO DECIMALS INTO PERCENTAGES

FRACTIONS, DECIMALS AND PERCENTAGES

$\frac{1}{2}$ is the same as 0.5, which is the same as 50%

$\frac{1}{4}$ is the same as 0.25, which is the same as 25%

$\frac{3}{4}$ is the same as 0.75, which is the same as 75%

$\frac{1}{5}$ is the same as 0.2, which is the same as 20%

$\frac{2}{5}$ is the same as 0.4, which is the same as 40%

$\frac{1}{10}$ is the same as 0.1, which is the same as 10%

CONVERT PERCENTAGES TO DECIMALS

- Divide the percentage by 100.

EXAMPLE

40% to a decimal = 40 ÷ 100 = 0.4

CONVERT DECIMALS TO PERCENTAGES

- Multiply the decimal by 100.

EXAMPLE

0.35 to a percentage = 0.35 x 100 = 35%

CONVERT FRACTIONS INTO PERCENTAGES

- Divide the top number of the fraction by the bottom number to give you the decimal and then multiply by 100 to give you the percentage.

EXAMPLE

¼ = 1 ÷ 4 = 0.25. To convert this to a percentage, multiply by 100 = 0.25 x 100 = 25%.

FRACTIONS, DECIMALS AND PERCENTAGES

CONVERT FRACTIONS INTO DECIMALS

- Divide the top number by the bottom number.

EXAMPLES

$$\frac{2}{10} = 2 \div 10 = 0.2 \qquad \frac{14}{100} = 14 \div 100 = 0.14$$

Now it's your turn! Convert these fractions into decimals

$$\frac{5}{10}$$

$$\frac{8}{10}$$

FRACTIONS, DECIMALS AND PERCENTAGES

CONVERT DECIMALS INTO FRACTIONS

- The digits after the decimal point will form the top part of your fraction.

- The bottom number of the fraction will need to be over 10, 100 or 1000.

EXAMPLE

This number will form the top part of the fraction!

$$0.124 = \frac{124}{\boxed{}} = \frac{124}{1000}$$

The bottom number will be 1000 because the decimal is representing 1 tenth, 2 hundreds and 4 thousandths.

You then need to work out whether the fraction will go over 10, 100 or 1000.

Now you try!

Write 0.46 as a fraction.

Write $\frac{456}{1000}$ as a decimal.

Question 1

Write this fraction as a decimal.

$\dfrac{1}{8}$ --------------------

Question 2

Write this fraction as a decimal.

$\dfrac{3}{5}$ --------------------

Question 3

Write this fraction as a decimal.

$\dfrac{2}{20}$ --------------------

Question 4

Write this fraction as a decimal.

$\dfrac{2}{3}$ --------------------

Question 5

Write this fraction as a decimal.

$\dfrac{7}{10}$ --------------------

Question 6

Write this fraction as a decimal.

$\dfrac{1}{1000}$ --------------------

Question 7

Write this fraction as a decimal.

$\dfrac{12}{100}$ --------------------

Question 8

Write this fraction as a decimal.

$\dfrac{6}{1000}$ --------------------

Question 9

Write this fraction as a decimal.

$\dfrac{1}{4}$ --------------------

Question 10

Write this fraction as a decimal.

$\dfrac{315}{1000}$ --------------------

Question 11

Write this fraction as a decimal.

$\dfrac{4}{20}$ --------------------

Question 12

Write this fraction as a decimal.

$\dfrac{22}{50}$ --------------------

Question 13

Write this fraction as a decimal.

$\dfrac{14}{25}$ --------------------

Question 14

Write this fraction as a decimal.

$\dfrac{9}{10}$ --------------------

Question 15

Write 0.208 as a fraction.

```
┌─────────┐
│         │
└─────────┘
┌─────────┐
│         │
└─────────┘
```

Question 16

Write 0.14 as a fraction.

```
┌─────────┐
│         │
└─────────┘
┌─────────┐
│         │
└─────────┘
```

Question 17

Write 0.53 as a fraction.

```
┌─────────┐
│         │
└─────────┘
┌─────────┐
│         │
└─────────┘
```

Question 18

Write 0.6 as a fraction.

```
┌─────────┐
│         │
└─────────┘
┌─────────┐
│         │
└─────────┘
```

Question 19

Write 0.215 as a fraction.

```
┌─────────┐
│         │
└─────────┘
┌─────────┐
│         │
└─────────┘
```

Question 20

Write 0.1 as a fraction.

```
┌─────────┐
│         │
└─────────┘
┌─────────┐
│         │
└─────────┘
```

Question 21

Write 0.156 as a fraction.

```
┌─────────┐
│         │
└─────────┘
┌─────────┐
│         │
└─────────┘
```

Question 22

Write 0.78 as a fraction.

```
┌─────────┐
│         │
└─────────┘
┌─────────┐
│         │
└─────────┘
```

Question 23

Write 0.12 as a fraction.

```
┌─────────┐
│         │
└─────────┘
┌─────────┐
│         │
└─────────┘
```

Question 24

Write 0.985 as a fraction.

```
┌─────────┐
│         │
└─────────┘
┌─────────┐
│         │
└─────────┘
```

Question 25

Write 0.1 as a percentage.

Question 26

Write 1/4 as a percentage.

Question 27

Write 3/4 as a percentage

Question 28

Write 0.35 as a percentage.

Question 29

Write 0.75 as a percentage.

Question 30

Write 0.2687 as a percentage.

Question 31

Write 40% as a decimal.

Question 32

Write 20% as a fraction.

Question 33

Write 1% as a decimal.

Question 34

Write 99% as a fraction.

ANSWERS TO FRACTIONS INTO DECIMALS INTO PERCENTAGES

Q1. 0.125

EXPLANATION = 1 ÷ 8 = 0.125

Q2. 0.6

EXPLANATION = 3 ÷ 5 = 0. 6

Q3. 0.1

EXPLANATION = 2 ÷ 20 = 0.1

Q4. 0.6666...

EXPLANATION = 2 ÷ 3 = 0.6666....

Q5. 0.7

EXPLANATION = 7 ÷ 10 = 0.7

Q6. 0.001

EXPLANATION = 1 ÷ 1000 = 0.001

Q7. 0.12

EXPLANATION = 12 ÷ 100 = 0.12

Q8. 0.006

EXPLANATION = 6 ÷ 1000 = 0.006

Q9. 0.25

EXPLANATION = 1 ÷ 4 = 0.25

Q10. 0.315

EXPLANATION = 315 ÷ 1000 = 0.315

Q11. 0.2

EXPLANATION = 4 ÷ 20 = 0.2

Q12. 0.44

EXPLANATION = 22 ÷ 50 = 0.44

Q13. 0.56

EXPLANATION = 14 ÷ 25 = 0.56

Q14. 0.9

EXPLANATION = 9 ÷ 10 = 0.9

Q15. $\dfrac{208}{1000} = \dfrac{26}{125}$

EXPLANATION = 0.208 = $\dfrac{208}{1000} = \dfrac{26}{125}$ (both numbers can be divided by 8).

Q16. $\dfrac{14}{100} = \dfrac{7}{50}$

EXPLANATION = 0.14 = $\dfrac{14}{100} = \dfrac{7}{50}$ (both numbers can be divided by 2).

Q17. $\dfrac{53}{100}$

EXPLANATION = 0.53 = $\dfrac{53}{100}$.

Q18. $\dfrac{6}{10} = \dfrac{3}{5}$

EXPLANATION = 0.6 = $\dfrac{6}{10} = \dfrac{3}{5}$ (both numbers can be divided by 2).

Q19. $\dfrac{215}{1000} = \dfrac{43}{200}$

EXPLANATION = 0.215 = $\dfrac{215}{1000} = \dfrac{43}{200}$ (both numbers can be divided by 5).

Q20. $\dfrac{1}{10}$

EXPLANATION = 0.1 = $\dfrac{1}{10}$

Q21. $\dfrac{156}{1000} = \dfrac{39}{250}$

EXPLANATION = 0.156 = $\dfrac{156}{1000} = \dfrac{39}{250}$ (both numbers can be divided by 4).

Q22. $\dfrac{78}{100} = \dfrac{39}{50}$

EXPLANATION = 0.78 = $\dfrac{78}{100} = \dfrac{39}{50}$ (both numbers can be divided by 2).

Q23. $\dfrac{12}{100} = \dfrac{3}{25}$

EXPLANATION = 0.12 = $\dfrac{12}{100} = \dfrac{6}{50} = \dfrac{3}{25}$ (both numbers can be divided by 4).

Q24. $\dfrac{985}{1000} = \dfrac{197}{200}$

EXPLANATION = 0.985 = $\dfrac{985}{1000} = \dfrac{197}{200}$ (both numbers can be divided by 5).

Q25. 10%

EXPLANATION = 0.1 as a percentage = 0.1 x 100 = 10%

Q26. 25%

EXPLANATION = $\dfrac{1}{4}$ as a percentage = 0.25 x 100 = 25%

Q27. 75%

EXPLANATION = $\dfrac{3}{4}$ as a percentage = 0.75 x 100 = 75%

Q28. 35%

EXPLANATION = 0.35 as a percentage = 0.35 x 100 = 35%

Q29. 75%

EXPLANATION = 0.75 as a percentage = 0.75 x 100 = 75%

Q30. 26.87%

EXPLANATION = 0.2687 as a percentage = 0.2687 x 100 = 26.87%

Q31. 0.4

EXPLANATION = 40% as a decimal = 40 ÷ 100 = 0.4

Q32. $\dfrac{1}{5}$

EXPLANATION = 20% as a fraction = $\dfrac{20}{100} = \dfrac{10}{50} = \dfrac{5}{25} = \dfrac{1}{5}$

Q33. 0.01

EXPLANATION = 1% as a decimal = 1 ÷ 100 = 0.01

Q34. $\dfrac{99}{100}$

EXPLANATION = 99% as a fraction = $\dfrac{99}{100}$

HOW ARE YOU GETTING ON?

THE
REVISION
SERIES

MOCK
TEST

Question 1

What fraction of the shape is shaded?

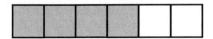

Question 2

What fraction of the shape is shaded?

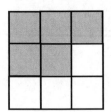

Question 3

Shade $\dfrac{1}{4}$ of the shape below.

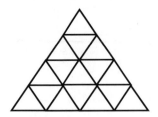

Question 4

Arrange these fractions from smallest to biggest.

$$\frac{3}{4} \quad \frac{7}{12} \quad \frac{1}{4} \quad \frac{7}{8}$$

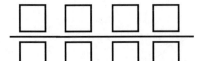

Question 5

Simplify these fractions.

a) $\dfrac{8}{16} \dfrac{\square}{\square}$

b) $\dfrac{9}{45} \dfrac{\square}{\square}$

c) $\dfrac{12}{36} \dfrac{\square}{\square}$

Question 6

Draw lines to join equivalent fractions. The first one has been done for you.

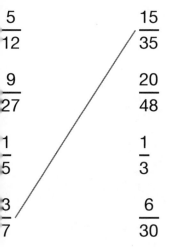

$\dfrac{5}{12}$	$\dfrac{15}{35}$
$\dfrac{9}{27}$	$\dfrac{20}{48}$
$\dfrac{1}{5}$	$\dfrac{1}{3}$
$\dfrac{3}{7}$	$\dfrac{6}{30}$

Question 7

Convert each of the following into a mixed fraction.

a) $\dfrac{15}{10} \ \square\dfrac{\square}{\square}$

b) $\dfrac{22}{11} \ \square\dfrac{\square}{\square}$

c) $\dfrac{36}{8} \ \square\dfrac{\square}{\square}$

Question 8

Circle the smallest fraction. Explain your reasons for this.

$$\frac{4}{10} \quad \frac{3}{5}$$

Question 9

Arrange these fractions from biggest to smallest.

$$\frac{2}{3} \quad \frac{1}{2} \quad \frac{3}{5} \quad \frac{4}{9}$$

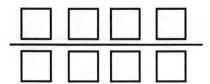

Question 10

Shade in $\dfrac{1}{5}$

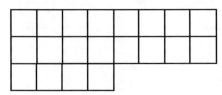

Question 11

What fraction of the shape is shaded in? Write your answer in its simplest form.

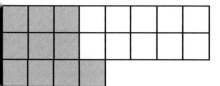

Question 12

Write $2\frac{3}{4}$ as an improper fraction. Show your workings out.

Answer

Question 13

Write 0.15 as a fraction.

Question 14

a)

0.45 + 0.983

b)

0.35 + 2.68

----

c)

5.68 – 2.47

d)

3.5 x 6.2

Question 15

The table below is not filled in completely. Complete the table. Give all fractions in their simplest form.

FRACTION	DECIMAL	PERCENTAGE
....	0.1	....
....	....	20%
$\frac{1}{2}$	....	....
....	0.75	....

Question 16

a)

$$\frac{1}{3} + \frac{3}{7} = \frac{\square}{\square}$$

b)

$$\frac{9}{12} - \frac{4}{12} = \frac{\square}{\square}$$

c)

$$\frac{1}{5} \div 2 = \frac{\square}{\square}$$

d)

$$\frac{1}{3} \times \frac{3}{4} = \frac{\square}{\square}$$

Question 17

Shade in 25% of the shape below.

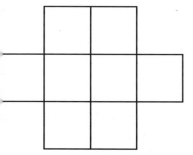

Question 18

Using the answer to question 17, what is this as a fraction?

Question 19

Out of the following, which would you rather have?

40% of £95?

1/5 of £150?

0.6 of £60?

Explain your answer.

Question 20

Work out what the missing number is.

$$33\% = \frac{\boxed{}}{\boxed{100}}$$

Question 21

Draw lines from each fraction to its equivalent percentage, and then draw a line to its equivalent decimal. The first one has been done for you.

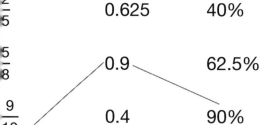

$\dfrac{2}{5}$

$\dfrac{5}{8}$

$\dfrac{9}{10}$

0.625   40%

0.9   62.5%

0.4   90%

Question 22

What percentage of the shape is shaded in? Write your answer in its simplest form.

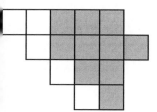

☐ %

Question 23

Change the following mixed fractions into improper fractions.

a) $1\dfrac{4}{9} = \dfrac{\square}{\square}$

b) $7\dfrac{3}{5} = \dfrac{\square}{\square}$

c) $13\dfrac{7}{9} = \dfrac{\square}{\square}$

Question 24

Grandpa Dan is telling you a story. When he was about 18 years old, he entered lots of competitions for the 200m sprint. He competed in 62 competitions altogether, before his injury. Out of all his competitions, he ranked 1st, 2nd or 3rd in 48 of them. What fraction is this? Give your answer in its simplest form.

Answer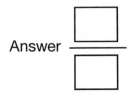

Question 25

Convert the following fraction into a decimal. Give your answer to 2 decimal places. Show your workings out in the box provided.

$$\frac{2}{7}$$

Answer:

Question 26

Using the signs <, > or =, place one of these between each pair of the following fractions.

a)

$$\frac{26}{40} \, \square \, \frac{18}{20}$$

b)

$$\frac{3}{4} \, \square \, \frac{2}{3}$$

Question 27

Round these decimals to one decimal place.

a)

36.43 ---------------------

b)

187.17 ---------------------

c)

86.19 ---------------------

d)

3.12 ---------------------

Question 28

Round these numbers up to the nearest whole number.

a)

1.7 ---------------------

b)

25.67 ---------------------

c)

5.4 ---------------------

d)

11.26 ---------------------

Question 29

Write these numbers in the correct position on the line below.

| -0.3 | 0.9 | 0.2 | 1.3 | -1.1 |

0

Question 30

Shade $\frac{5}{8}$ of the shape below.

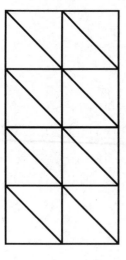

ANSWERS TO MOCK TEST

Q1. $\dfrac{4}{6}$ or $\dfrac{2}{3}$

EXPLANATION = there are 6 squares in total. This forms the bottom part of the fraction (denominator). 4 squares are shaded in. This forms the top part of the fraction (numerator). That gives you the fraction of $\dfrac{4}{6}$. This fraction can be simplified to $\dfrac{2}{3}$ (both the top number and bottom number can be divided by 2).

Q2. $\dfrac{5}{9}$

EXPLANATION = there are 9 squares in total. This forms the bottom part of the fraction (denominator). 5 squares are shaded in. This forms the top part of the fraction (numerator). That gives you the fraction of $\dfrac{5}{9}$.

Q3. Your answer should look like this:

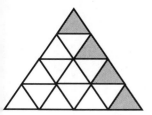

Q4. $\dfrac{1}{4}, \dfrac{7}{12}, \dfrac{3}{4}, \dfrac{7}{8}$

EXPLANATION = you would need to find the least common denominator (which is 24). Rewrite these fractions as equivalent fractions, using 24 as the bottom number. Multiply the top number of the fraction by whatever number you used to get 24 for the bottom.

$\dfrac{18}{24}, \dfrac{14}{24}, \dfrac{6}{24}, \dfrac{21}{24}$ = All you would have to do now is rearrange them from smallest to biggest.

Q5 a) $\dfrac{1}{2}$

EXPLANATION = $\dfrac{8}{16}$ both numbers can be divided by 8.

b) $\dfrac{1}{5}$

EXPLANATION $= \dfrac{9}{45}$ both numbers can be divided by 9.

c) $\dfrac{1}{3}$

EXPLANATION $= \dfrac{12}{36}$ both numbers can be divided by 12.

Q6. Your answer should look like this:

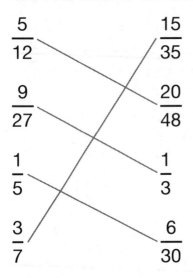

$\dfrac{5}{12}$	$\dfrac{15}{35}$
$\dfrac{9}{27}$	$\dfrac{20}{48}$
$\dfrac{1}{5}$	$\dfrac{1}{3}$
$\dfrac{3}{7}$	$\dfrac{6}{30}$

Q7 a) $1\dfrac{5}{10}$

EXPLANATION = 10 goes in to 15 = 1 time. Therefore 1 would be the whole number. After you put 10 into 15, find the remainder = 15 − 10 = 5. That forms the top part of the fraction. The bottom number remains the same.

b) 2

EXPLANATION = 11 goes in to 22 = twice. Therefore 2 would be the whole number. There is no remainder, so we don't need to write a fraction.

c) $4\dfrac{4}{8}$ or $4\dfrac{1}{2}$

EXPLANATION = 8 goes into 36 = 4 times. Therefore 4 would be the whole number. Now find the remainder = 36 − 32 = 4. That forms the top part of the fraction. The bottom number remains the same.

Q8. $\dfrac{4}{10}$

EXPLANATION = $\dfrac{4}{10}$ is the smallest out of the two fractions. The reason for this is because if you simplify $\dfrac{4}{10}$ (divide both numbers by 2), you will get $\dfrac{2}{5}$. This fraction is smaller than $\dfrac{3}{5}$.

Q9. $\dfrac{2}{3}$, $\dfrac{3}{5}$, $\dfrac{1}{2}$, $\dfrac{4}{9}$

EXPLANATION = you would need to find the least common denominator (which is 90). Rewrite these fractions as equivalent fractions, using 90 as the bottom number. Multiply the top number of the fraction by whatever number you used to get 90 for the bottom.

$\dfrac{60}{90}$, $\dfrac{45}{90}$, $\dfrac{54}{90}$, $\dfrac{40}{90}$ = All you would have to do now is rearrange them from biggest to smallest.

Q10. Your answer should look something like this:

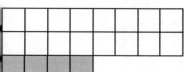

Q11. $\dfrac{1}{2}$

EXPLANATION = there are 20 squares in total. 10 of them are shaded in. That has the fraction of $\dfrac{10}{20}$. In its simplest form, both numbers can be divided by 10 = $\dfrac{1}{2}$.

Q12. $\dfrac{11}{4}$

EXPLANATION = your fraction will have the denominator of 4. There are 4 quarters in one whole. So 4 x 2 = 8 quarters (there are 8 quarters in the 2 wholes). Add on the extra 3 quarters = 8 + 3 = 11.

Q13. $\dfrac{15}{100} = \dfrac{3}{20}$

EXPLANATION = 0.15 = $\dfrac{15}{100} = \dfrac{3}{20}$ (both numbers can be divided by 5).

Q14. A) 1.433

EXPLANATION = 0.45 + 0.983 = 1.433

   B) 3.03

EXPLANATION = 0.35 + 2.68 = 3.03

   C) 3.21

EXPLANATION = 5.68 − 2.47 = 3.21

   D) 21.7

EXPLANATION = 3.5 x 6.2. Remove the decimal points, do the multiplication, and then add in the decimal points at the end. So, 35 x 62 = 2170. Now add in the decimal point. There are two numbers that need to be after the decimal point (.5 and .2). So 2170 becomes 21.70 or 21.7

Q15. Your answer should look like this:

FRACTION	DECIMAL	PERCENTAGE
$\dfrac{1}{10}$	0.1	**10%**
$\dfrac{1}{5}$	**0.2**	20%
$\dfrac{1}{2}$	**0.5**	**50%**
$\dfrac{3}{4}$	0.75	**75%**

Q16. A) $\dfrac{16}{21}$

EXPLANATION $= \dfrac{1}{3} + \dfrac{3}{7} = \dfrac{7+9}{21} = \dfrac{16}{21}$

B) $\dfrac{5}{12}$

EXPLANATION = $\dfrac{\cancel{9}}{12} - \dfrac{\cancel{4}}{12} = \dfrac{5}{12}$

C) $\dfrac{1}{10}$

EXPLANATION = $\dfrac{1}{5} \div \dfrac{2}{1} = \dfrac{1}{5} \times \dfrac{1}{2} = \dfrac{1}{10}$

D) $\dfrac{3}{12} = \dfrac{1}{4}$

EXPLANATION = $\dfrac{1}{3} \times \dfrac{3}{4} = \dfrac{3}{12} = \dfrac{1}{4}$

Q17. Your answer should look something like this:

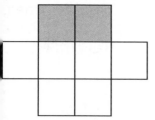

Q18. $\dfrac{1}{4}$

EXPLANATION = using the answer to question 17, 25% as a fraction is $\dfrac{1}{4}$.
(100 ÷ 25 = 4). Therefore there are 4 equal sections to every whole (100%).

Q19. 40% of £95

EXPLANATION = your answer should read something like this: '*I would rather have 40% of £95, because this is more money. 40% of £95 is 95 ÷ 100 x 40 = £38.*

1/5 of £150 is 150 ÷ 5 = £30. To work out 0.6 of £60 = 0.6 x 100 = 60%. So, £60 ÷ 100 x 60 = £36. Therefore 40% of £95 is more.

Q20. 33

EXPLANATION = 33% is equivalent to 33 out of 100.

Q21. Your answer should look something like this:

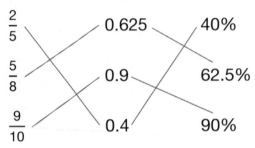

$\dfrac{2}{5}$ 0.625   40%

$\dfrac{5}{8}$ 0.9   62.5%

$\dfrac{9}{10}$ 0.4   90%

Q22. 50%

EXPLANATION = there are 20 squares in total, 10 of which are shaded. Therefore this can be represented by the fraction of 10/20 or 1/2. To work out the percentage, you need to know the equivalent to 1/2. Half of 100(%) is 50%.

Q23. A) $\dfrac{13}{9}$

EXPLANATION = to convert $1\dfrac{4}{9}$ into an improper fraction:

Step 1 = 1 x 9 = 9

Step 2 = 9 + 4 = 13

Step 3 = the number on bottom of the fraction will remain the same = 9

Step 4 = $\dfrac{13}{9}$

B) $\dfrac{38}{5}$

EXPLANATION = to convert $7\dfrac{3}{5}$ into an improper fraction:

Step 1 = 7 x 5 = 35

Step 2 = 35 + 3 = 38

Step 3 = the number on bottom of the fraction will remain the same = 5

Step 4 = $\dfrac{38}{5}$

C) $\dfrac{124}{9}$

EXPLANATION = to convert $13\,\dfrac{7}{9}$ into an improper fraction:

Step 1 = 13 x 9 = 117

Step 2 = 117 + 7 = 124

Step 3 = the number on bottom of the fraction will remain the same = 9

Step 4 = $\dfrac{124}{9}$

Q24. 24/31

EXPLANATION = Grandpa Dan ranked 1st, 2nd or 3rd in 48 out of 62 competitions. This can be written in the fraction of $\dfrac{48}{62}$. In its simplest form, it can be simplified to $\dfrac{24}{31}$ (both numbers from the original fraction can be divided by 2).

Q25. 0.29

EXPLANATION = to convert $\dfrac{2}{7}$ into a decimal, you need to divide the top number by the bottom number. 2÷ 7 = 0.285... Remember, the question asks you to give your answer to 2 decimal places, so 0.285 will become 0.29. The second number after the decimal point is 8. Using the next number, the '5', you need to round up or round down. If the number is 5 or above, then you will round the 8 up.

Q26. a) <

EXPLANATION = $\dfrac{26}{40}$ and $\dfrac{18}{20}$. Change the fractions, so that they both have the same bottom number. $\dfrac{26}{40}$ and $\dfrac{36}{40}$ (if you doubled the second fraction, that would give you the same bottom number). Therefore this demonstrates that the second fraction is in fact bigger.

b) >

EXPLANATION = $\dfrac{3}{4}$ and $\dfrac{2}{3}$. Change the fractions, so that they both have the same bottom number. $\dfrac{9}{12}$ and $\dfrac{8}{12}$ (you need to find an equivalent fraction, whereby both fractions have the same bottom number). Therefore this demonstrates that the first fraction is in fact bigger.

Q27. a) 36.4

   b) 187.2

   c) 86.2

   d) 3.1

Q28. a) 2

   b) 26

   c) 5

   d) 11

Q29. Your answer should look something like this:

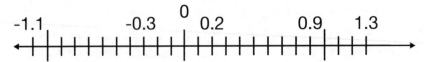

Q30. Your answer should look something like this:

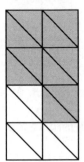

HOW ARE YOU GETTING ON?